CW01635211

The Jennifer O'Reilly Memorial Lecture

IONA

The Jennifer O'Reilly Memorial Lecture Series

The Memorial Lecture in honour of Jennifer O'Reilly was established in 2017 by the School of History, University College Cork. Each year a distinguished scholar is invited to speak on either the age of Bede or medieval iconography, two subjects that Dr O'Reilly explored in her research and teaching.

2017 On Bede and Cassiodorus
Dr Alan Thacker, the Institute of Historical Research.

2018 Venerating the Cross around the year 800 in Anglo-Saxon England
Professor Jane Hawkes, University of York.

2019 At the Ends of the Earth: Conversion and its consequences in some Insular Sources
Professor Máire Herbert, University College Cork.

2020 The Early Medieval Eye and Insular Art: The Codex Amiatinus, the Book of Kells, and the scholarship of Jennifer O'Reilly
Dr Carol A. Farr, University of London.

2021 Dynamic Theologies: The Ruthwell Cross from an Irish perspective
Professor Éamonn Ó Carragáin, University College Cork.

2022 Bede and the Spiritual Senses
Professor Arthur Holder, Graduate Theological Union.

2023 *Pater* Ecgberct of Rathmelsigi: The hero of Bede's *Historia Ecclesiastica*?
Professor Dáibhí Ó Cróinín, University of Galway.

Photo: © Dermot Roantree

Dr Jennifer O'Reilly (1943–2016)

Remembered as a gifted lecturer and writer by her colleagues and her students, Dr Jennifer O'Reilly played a key role in establishing the degree programme in History of Art at UCC, where she lectured on medieval history between 1975 and her retirement in 2008. Her scholarly interests and publications lay principally in three areas: the iconography of early Irish and Anglo-Saxon art; the writings of Bede the Venerable and Adomnán of Iona; and medieval hagiography. In these areas she explored the intimate relations between medieval texts and images and the traditions of biblical exegesis shaped by the Church Fathers. Her teaching inspired generations of students, many of whom went on to complete doctorates under her supervision. In retirement she continued to write extensively, and she gave numerous public lectures, including the Jarrow Lecture and the Brixworth Lecture. She was a Member of the Royal Irish Academy and a Fellow of the Society of Antiquaries.

Iona is an imprint of Prosperity Education Limited
Registered offices: 58 Sherlock Close, Cambridge CB3 0HP,
United Kingdom

First published 2021

Typesetting and cover design by ORP Cambridge

To view the full-colour plate section:

- Go to url www.prosperityeducation.net/2018-memorial-lecture-images
- Password: Iona2018
- Select the book image
- Select content to download

A catalogue record for this book is available from the British Library

ISBN: 978-1-913825-97-3

For further information visit:
www.ucc.ie/en/history/drjenniferoreillymemorialpage

The recorded Jennifer O'Reilly Memorial Lectures are available on YouTube.

Printed and Kindle editions of the Jennifer O'Reilly Memorial Lectures are available on Amazon.

The Jennifer O'Reilly
Memorial Lecture
2018

Venerating the Cross around the year 800 in Anglo-Saxon England

Jane Hawkes

Venerating the Cross around the year 800 in Anglo-Saxon England

The year I started my doctorate an article appeared in the *Journal of the Warburg and Courtauld Institutes* co-authored by Jennifer O'Reilly and Elizabeth Okasha on the late Anglo-Saxon portable altar now housed at the Musée de Cluny in Paris (Fig. 1).[1] It was, inevitably, one of the first things I read, particularly in the light of the task that had been assigned me by my supervisor: the iconographic significance of the late eighth-century Rothbury Cross from Northumberland which displays the figure of the Crucified in the cross-head (Fig. 2). Unsurprisingly, in this context, Jennifer's comments on what she called the "abbreviated crucifixion" on the Cluny Altar proved to be of great interest. Most arresting was her argument that although the victorious Christ awake on the cross had begun to yield to the image of the dead Christ during the late tenth and early eleventh century in Anglo-Saxon art, the version on the Altar, produced at an advanced stage in this transition, yet depicted a figure expressing resignation rather than anguish. Life, death, suffering, anguish and resignation:[2] the possibilities inherent in a single image-type that were opened up by this argument were truly daunting to a first-year PhD student; and so they remain.

Yet, as a tribute to Jennifer and her work all these years later, I would like to offer some observations on the Crucifixion articulated in the iconography of the monumental stone crosses set up across the Anglo-Saxon landscape around the year 800: at the time when the 'victorious Christ alive on the cross' was the established mode of presentation in north-western Europe, although the initial phases of the transition that Jennifer discussed were beginning to appear.

The High Cross in Anglo-Saxon England

Being unique to the Insular world until at least the late eleventh/twelfth century, the large-scale public sculptural form of the high cross has attracted considerable scholarly attention for some time

(Fig. 3), but increasingly so since the early twentieth century. Given its distinctive 'free-standing' form, attempts to explain its emergence in Anglo-Saxon England have resulted in a general understanding of it as an innovation reflecting the amalgamation of a number of material and cultural phenomena.

Perhaps foremost among these is the fact that the crosses reflect the re-invigoration of the art of stone sculpture following the re-establishment of the Christian Church in the region during the course of the seventh century when, as Bede records in his *Ecclesiastical History*, churches began to be constructed in stone and were decorated and furnished with carved stone work.[3] Related to this, but in a different medium, was the practice of erecting wooden crosses in monasteries in the Irish world: such as the crosses set up on Iona to mark sites associated with Columba as recorded by Adomnán in his *Life* of the saint; and that erected by Oswald in an act of Constantinian imitation prior to his victorious engagement with Caedwalla at Heavenfield on his return from Iona in the early seventh century.[4]

In their design the stone monuments also seem to represent the influence of earlier, late antique and early Christian monumental forms: the triumphal column and the obelisk. The first of these, the stone column, was a form that was associated, at the time, with the triumphal sign of the cross encountered in Constantinian contexts in the early Christian Mediterranean world: in Jerusalem, where a (triumphal) column is recorded as having been surmounted by a cross and carved with a *Maiestas* near the top which stood close to the Holy Sepulchre complex.[5] Although this monument is unlikely to have been physically encountered by Anglo-Saxons (other than Willibald whose travels to Jerusalem were recorded in the eighth century),[6] the forms of the triumphal and Jupiter columns would have been familiar across Europe and in Rome. Together, associations and encounters with the circular columns of antiquity are likely to have informed that of the monumental columns supporting crosses that featured the *Maiestas* in their upper registers – which were set up at the turn of the ninth century in Anglo-Saxon England.[7] The second monumental form, the obelisk, is now generally understood to have informed that of the more familiar slightly tapering, squared-shaft of the high crosses: the obelisk shaft being surmounted by a cross-head in its rearticulated incarnation. In this instance, familiarity with the monument that stood to the south of Old St Peter's in Rome where it originally marked the point of Peter's martyrdom (Fig. 4), would have rendered the squared tapering form of the cross-shaft particularly emotive.[8]

At a less formalist level, the introduction of the cult of the cross into the region at the turn of the eighth century seems also to have played a part in the sources of inspiration informing the development of the monumental high cross, particularly, as Éamonn Ó Carragáin has argued, following the recovery of a fragment of the True Cross in Rome by Pope Sergius and the introduction of the feast of the True Cross at the turn of the eighth century.[9] Richard Bailey has further pointed to the importance of the idea of the eschatological *crux gemmata*, perhaps inspired in part by knowledge of the gemmed cross set up by Theodosius II (reg. 408–450) on the altar of the True Cross in the Sepulchre complex in Jerusalem.[10] In this respect, the stone crosses can be understood to represent (in materially permanent form) the wooden crosses enshrined in jewel-encrusted precious metals familiar in processions and on altars, their placement sacralising the landscape. Here, it is worth noting that the jewelled crosses familiar in the context of ecclesiastical ritual were not designed as crucifixes; all were *crux gemmata* (Fig. 5). Indeed, early depictions of the Crucifixion did not necessarily even illustrate the cross behind the figure of the Crucified – as is the case with the fifth-century carved wooden panel set in the doors of the church of Santa Sabina in Rome (Fig. 6).[11]

Furthermore, it has become increasingly apparent that the high crosses of early Christian Anglo-Saxon England, although monumental and decorated in relief carving, were also brightly painted and multi-media in their presentation: inset with glass and metal. Traces of polychromy have been noted on a number of stone crosses,[12] and the more recently recovered fragments of the early ninth-century stone shrine built to encase the wooden reliquary chest containing the remains of St Chad at Lichfield demonstrate the nature of such colouration (Fig. 7). Forming one half of the gabled end of the house-shaped shrine the ground was painted white and framed in red, with the figure of the Archangel Gabriel wearing a yellow robe under-painted with red hatching to replicate the red-gold colour (Old English: *raed*) so prized by Anglo-Saxons. The feathers of his wings are likewise rendered in a sophisticated painterly manner, each feather painted red, shaded through pink to white. An oil-based paint was used for the halo and flecks of gold foil once adhered to it.[13]

Elsewhere there is evidence that the carvings were enhanced with the addition of metal and paste-glass insets. One fragment of the *c.* 800 column from Reculver (Kent) depicting the Ascension, for instance, shows signs of a metal staff-cross held by the ascending Christ – in addition to the red paint preserved in the background and the blue used for Christ's robes (Fig. 8);[14] the central boss of the cross-head surmounting the early ninth-century cross that stands in the market place at Sandbach in Cheshire is surrounded at equidistant points by small drilled holes used to attach a metal collar or cover around the boss;[15] and the deeply drilled eyes of figures, such as those on the Rothbury Cross, testify to the paste-glass that once filled them.[16] Recent restoration of the fragment from Aberlady, East Lothian, has also revealed the tin casing inserted into just such holes intended to hold the paste glass in place.[17]

Thus, overall, the Anglo-Saxon high cross, being rendered in stone, has come to be regarded as visually presenting, in a monumental and permanent manner, the eternal imperium of the Church and the Heavenly Jerusalem: as making permanent in the landscape, that which was represented temporally (in terms of their medium), by the metalwork crosses within the churches.

This said, however, it is notable that between the eighth through ninth centuries these monuments, like their metalwork counterparts, did not tend to function as crucifixes or roods; they did not reproduce the image of the crucifixion in the cross-head. The Rothbury Crucifixion (Fig. 2) is in fact one of only two exceptions to this general trend. Despite the fact that it survives as a fragment, it preserves the arm of the Crucified in the one extant horizontal cross-arm and his head in the upper vertical cross-arm, over which a (moustachioed) angel descends to clasp Christ's triple-cruciform halo, physically presenting the magisterial triumph achieved through his victory over death at the crucifixion. Here the intimations of death are indicated by the ever so slightly drooping angle of the hand – an early glimpse of that transition from Christ living on the cross to suffering and dying upon it.[18] The other exception is the badly damaged scheme found at

Bakewell in Derbyshire (Fig. 9). Here, part of a narrative scene of the Crucifixion fills what remains of the upper reaches of the cross-shaft and cross-head. Christ on the cross is flanked by Stephaton and Longinus while the cross itself is set within a cross-hatched mound representing Golgotha.[19] Apart from these two exceptions the general rule in the pre-Viking period was to place the image of the Crucifixion on the shaft of the monumental cross, as is the case at Sandbach, for instance.[20] In some cases, however, the scheme was set at the base of the shaft: as at Hexham, Northumberland (mid-eighth century), or at Bradbourne in Derbyshire, in the early ninth century (Figs 10, 12).[21]

Venerating the Cross

These carvings are particularly interesting in what they reveal about attitudes to the public display of the crucifixion in early Christian Anglo-Saxon England. At Hexham, Christ, flanked by Stephaton and Longinus, wears a short loincloth and sports a prominent dished halo. The lower cross-arm continues below the wide flat horizontal moulding that traverses it, into the mound of Golgotha (Fig. 10). Above Christ, apparently uniquely in the extant corpus of early Christian art, a large medallion is set over the upper vertical cross-arm. Only the faint remains of what was once carved in very low relief on its surface are preserved: insufficient to draw any clear conclusions about what it once displayed. It is hard to imagine a single medallion containing the symbols of both the heavenly bodies, but it is not impossible to postulate that it might have displayed the *Manus Dei*. Although not included in images of the Crucifixion the Hand of God was integral to schemes featuring Christ in Majesty where it was framed within a wreath or crown bestowed by the Father on the Son. The apse mosaic in San Stefano Rotondo, dated to the pontificate of Theodore I (642–649), for instance, depicts the Hand of God clasping a laurel wreath of immortality emerging from a starred hemisphere over the bust of Christ set in a medallion surmounting the *crux gemmata* (Fig. 11). Produced less than a decade before Anglo-Saxon ecclesiasts first travelled to Rome this iconographic scheme speaks to the majesty of Christ gained through the salvation won at the Crucifixion.[22] While it cannot be demonstrated unequivocally that the *Manus Dei* was similarly disposed above the nimbed head of Christ on the cross at Hexham, this frame of reference would not be irrelevant within the context of an image of the crucifixion where Christ does not hang on the cross, but stands triumphant in the death that was understood to be the means to everlasting life. Christ himself is disposed upright on the cross with his arms extended at right-angles to his body, his head three-quarter turned to his right towards the spear-bearer, but not bowed. Presented at eye-level for anyone kneeling or prostrating themselves before the stone cross at Hexham, therefore, the panel displays Christ crucified on a cross set within the mound of Golgotha over which he stands triumphant and possibly crowned with immortality by the Hand of God, recalling the text of Philippians 2:8–10:

> He humbled himself, becoming obedient unto death, even to the death of the cross. For which cause God also hath exalted him, and hath given him a name which is above all names: That in the name of Jesus every knee should bow, of those that are in heaven, on earth, and under the earth.[23]

Although Bede did not write a commentary on this epistle he did adapt the selection of Augustine's writings that had been compiled by Eugippius (*c.* 460–535) in his monastery in Naples (Casatellum Lucullanum), which included Augustine's commentary on Paul's letter to the Philippians.[24] This focussed on the humiliation that Christ endured in his death on the cross, which Augustine, followed by Bede, designated *tropaeum* (trophy) a word that denoted, in imperial contexts, a sign and memorial of martial victory, originally formed from the trunk of a tree and later made into stone and ornamented. It is worth noting in this context that the laurel wreath awarded such victors signified the gift of eternal life earned by their actions and so was adopted early into Christian art with this signfication. Thus, both Augustine and Bede noted in closing their commentary on Philippians 2:8, citing Paul's letter to the Galatians 6:14 that: "I should glory [only] in the cross of our Lord Jesus Christ", the means of the Crucifixion.[25]

At Bradbourne, the iconographic emphasis differs (Fig. 12). While Christ stands against the cross wearing a short loincloth, flanked by Stephaton and Longinus (as at Hexham), above the horizontal cross-arms are medallions containing the symbols of the sun and moon, and deeply drilled holes pierce his hands and feet, as well as the eyes of all three figures. While it is possible to imagine paste glass in the eyes, it may well be that metal insets were placed in the hands and feet of the Crucified recreating the nails understood to have been used at the crucifixion. The iconographic significance of this feature would have complemented the figures of Longinus and Stephaton in keeping with the increased emphasis placed on Christ's humanity at the Crucifixion, this suffering, and the redemptive nature of the event, confirmed at each re-enactment of the Eucharist, at the turn of the ninth century.[26]

Attitudes to the Crucifixion at this time, however, as intimated in the earlier Hexham panel – and at Rothbury – remained concerned to highlight Christ's divinity, and it was this that resulted in the re-introduction and prominence given to the symbols of the sun and moon included in depictions of the Crucifixion – as seen in the Carolingian ivories.[27] While these sometimes function as symbols of the darkness that fell over the face of the earth at the ninth hour, their presence was more usually intended to symbolise the cosmic nature of Christ's divine sovereignty, and in Carolingian art they were used as 'heavenly' witnesses to the divinity that made possible the victory over death at the Crucifixion and the promise of resurrection and everlasting life.[28] Their prominence in the Bradbourne scene, along with that given to the nails piercing Christ's hands, point to the influence of such images and the liturgical responses lying behind them that were current from the early ninth century onwards.

Providing further insight into how such an image might have functioned, is the Crucifixion at Bakewell, produced by the same centre responsible for that at Bradbourne.[29] The upper reaches of the image have been lost by the break in the stone but, as already noted, it preserves the sponge- and spear-bearers, and the lower beam of the crucifix inserted, almost in 'cross-section', into the Hill of Golgotha. This is a detail that was present in Anglo-Saxon art by the eighth century (being included in the Hexham panel),[30] but it gained greater currency in the Carolingian world during the ninth century; it was intended to highlight the association of the Crucifixion with Golgotha, that geographical point understood to mark the centre of the world and the site to which Christ would return at the Second Coming.[31] Other features, such as the use of the loincloth type of

Christ and the presence of Longinus and Stephaton were intended to highlight the humanity of Christ at his sacrifice, augmenting the allusions made by Christ's naked torso, the bleeding of the wound inflicted by the spear, and the suffering implied by the vinegar-soaked sponge. At another level, however, the spear-bearer also served to refer to the Old Testament prophecy by Zechariah (12:10) of the piercing of the Messiah:

> And I will pour out upon the house of David, and upon the inhabitants of Jerusalem, the spirit of grace, and of prayers: *and they shall look upon me, whom they have pierced*: and they shall mourn for him as one mourneth for an only son, and they shall grieve over him, as the manner is to grieve for the death of the firstborn (emphasis added).[32]

In early exegesis this was commonly associated with the exalted Christ of Revelation 1:7, which describes how, as Christ descends in the clouds "every eye shall see him, and they also that pierced him".[33] Thus, in his homily on John 8:15–18 (on Christ's discussion with the Pharisees on judgement), Augustine links Christ's return at the Second Coming – foretold at his Ascension (Acts 1:9–11) – with Zechariah's prophecy:

> The Son alone will be apparent to the good and the bad in the judgment in the form in which he suffered and rose again and ascended into heaven [...]. That is, in the form of man in which he was judged, [he] will be judge, in order that also that prophetic utterance may be fulfilled, "They shall look upon him whom they pierced".[34]

The association was also made in discussions of baptism in that the wound (the piercing of the spear-bearer) was regarded as a source of life shared by the baptised. Thus, in another homily on John (on the Crucifixion, burial and Resurrection), Augustine links the piercing of Christ's side with the waters of baptism:

> "One of the soldiers with a spear laid open his side and forthwith came thereout blood and water." A suggestive word was made use of by the evangelist in not saying pierced [...] but "opened" that

> thereby, in a sense, the gate of life might be thrown open from whence have flowed forth the sacraments of the Church without which there is no entrance to the life which is the true life.[35]

The scene at Bakewell therefore, although incomplete, preserves elements that point to a complex set of references incorporating the human and redemptive aspects of the Crucifixion, the mysteries of the Eucharist and Baptism, and the General Resurrection of the Dead at the Second Coming at which time Christ will appear in magisterial triumph.[36]

This is enhanced even further, however, by the pair of figures in the panel that follows (Fig. 13a–b). While they have been explained as Mary and Elizabeth of the Visitation, their attitude suggests they might be better identified as a pair of figures venerating the Crucifixion above. The iconography of the Visitation during the early middle ages conformed to two specific types: Embracing and Conversing. The former is most famously featured in an eighth-century Anglo-Saxon context on the upper stone of the Ruthwell Cross in Dumfriesshire (Fig. 14a), but it is also found on the contemporary ivory Genoels-Elderen diptych now in Brussels.[37] The Conversing type is found in the early ninth century at Hovingham, in Yorkshire (Fig. 14b).[38] Neither of these distinctive iconographic types, however, conforms to the attitude of the figures at Bakewell whose bodies do not embrace, and whose arms, while raised, do not indicate conversation. Rather, the way their upper bodies incline towards the centre of the panel, and their arms extend up towards the panel above, as well as the way their heads appear to be tipped back, looking up at the Crucifixion, are details that together suggest the figures can be understood to venerate Christ on the cross.

This said, figures adoring Christ in this manner are not a common feature of Christian art of the early medieval period. When the liturgical ritual of the *adoratio crucis* was illustrated (as a feature of early/mid-ninth-century Carolingian art) the adoring figures were depicted kneeling, as required in the Good Friday liturgy – and as might have been enacted before the Crucifixion panel at the base of the cross-shaft at Bradbourne (Fig. 15).[39] From the turn of the ninth century onwards, however, figures depicted standing at the foot of the cross (generally, but not always Mary and John), tend to have their arms extended towards the cross in exaggerated gestures indicative of their role as witnesses, rather than mourners as was traditional in earlier Crucifixion iconography.[40] It is an attitude that, as Celia Chazelle has demonstrated, reflected the increased emphasis placed on the veneration of both Christ and the cross (in the visual arts) as signs of the redemptive nature of the Crucifixion during the course of the ninth century.[41] The presence of a pair of figures with their arms upraised, and their heads upturned towards the Crucifixion in the upper reaches of the cross-shaft at Bakewell can thus be understood, in an early ninth-century context, as reflecting the iconographies of either the *adoratio crucis* (with the figures standing in adoration rather than kneeling), or bearing witness to the salvific nature of Christ, the cross and the Crucifixion.

If the figures were intended to depict the *adoratio crucis*, their setting within the panel below the Crucifixion (Fig. 13a), likely dictated by the confines of the monument, would have rendered their iconographic significance unclear if they had been depicted as kneeling; this pose would have removed them from the foot of the crucifix, the reference point of the ritual. However, standing with their heads and arms raised towards the cross, preserves the iconographic function of the *adoratio*, whilst also incorporating reference to the increased importance given to witnessing the redemptive nature of the Crucifixion, and emphasising the role of sight in inspiring the compunction leading to contemplation.[42] Considered in this way the panel thus forces the eyes of the viewer up in imitation of the pose of the two adoring or venerating figures, to the Crucifixion scene in the upper reaches of the cross, into the cross-head itself. Set almost at head height, the position of these two figures encourages – indeed emulates – the viewer in the act of contemplation: of the form of the cross itself, and of its varied significations in Christian and ecclesiastical frames of reference.

Contemplating the Cross

With this in mind it is perhaps worth turning, in closing, to consider the ways in which the viewer might have been encouraged in their act of contemplating the cross when confronted with images, such as the Crucifixion, presented on the surface of these monumental sculptures. As noted, these carvings tended to be brightly coloured and inset with paste metal and glass. Arranged in frames up the length of the shaft, or enclosed within the cross-head, they thus functioned as painted panels – a vertical iconostasis to paraphrase John Mitchell – but with the 'added extra' of being presented in three-dimensions.[43] The bright colours and (occasionally) glittering nature of the free-standing monumental crosses would have had the immediate effect of making them highly visible and immediate to those encountering them. This is perhaps best exemplified by the Rothbury Cross which preserves holes in the arms of its cross-head which held candles or floating wicks (Fig. 2). Here, standing within the church, the effect of glittering candlelight would have lent considerable impact to the carvings on the monument, not least of which is the visceral representation of the Damned in Hell at the base of the shaft, the paste-glass eyes reflecting light from the cross-head above, and the naked genitalia of the Damned threatened by the jaws of the serpentine creatures whose coils entrap them and whose eyes would also have glinted in the light (Fig. 16). The carvings would thus have presented a series of clearly visible images covering the surfaces of the monuments, the colours guiding the viewing experiences and facilitating understanding, in a fairly immediate way, of the significances of that which was being scrutinised.

More than this, however, as I have argued elsewhere, the panelled arrangement of these poly-chromed carvings suggests that they were intended to function in a manner analogous to painted wooden panels: today referred to as 'icons'.[44] Such images would have been encountered by Anglo-Saxon visitors to Rome and were familiar in the region both in Canterbury (where a panel painting of Christ was processed into the city by Augustine and his mission in 597), and in Northumbria, where they were displayed in Benedict Biscop's churches at Jarrow and Wearmouth.[45] Indeed, Bede himself makes the association between the painted wooden panel and sculptural panel in his commentary on the Temple where he turns to justify the use of images in sacred settings, and does so through the examples he saw before him on a daily basis.[46] He concludes this passage with a rhetorical question:

> if it was not contrary to that same law [of the Old Testament] to make historiated sculptures [those that furnished the Temple]

> why should it be contrary to the law *to sculpture or to paint as panels* the stories of the saints and martyrs of Christ, who by their observance of the divine law, have earned the glory of an eternal reward? (emphasis added)[47]

Clearly, for Bede colour, paint, wooden panels and carved images were all interchangeable, being part of the visual world with which he was familiar. In other words, sculptured stone panels and painted wooden panels were synonymous with each other, implying that the painted panels carved in relief that were presented on the monumental crosses were likely to have functioned in a manner analogous to that associated with the painted wooden panels we refer to as 'icons'. What this tells us is that while there was some familiarity with panel paintings they were also expected to function as objects inducing compunction and so inspiring contemplation – the requisite attitude for achieving understanding of salvation. For, as Bede went on to argue in his commentary on the Temple in respect of images of the Crucifixion, repeating what he had said in his History of the Abbots:

> if it was permissible to create and view elaborate visuals in the Temple, surely it was within the law to display panel paintings in a church because "their sight is wont [...] to produce a feeling of great *compunction* in the beholder" (emphasis added).[48]

In this he was, of course, writing within the tradition articulated by Gregory the Great a century earlier, a tradition that was still current in the works of Bede's contemporary, John of Damascus. In his letter to Serenus, the Bishop of Marseilles, in 601, Gregory had argued strenuously that the clergy be encouraged to make it clear to the congregation:

> that from the sight of the event portrayed [in the image] they should catch *the ardor of compunction*, and bow themselves down in adoration of the One Almighty Holy Trinity (emphasis added).[49]

While Bede may not have been familiar with this letter, he was nevertheless responding to the iconoclastic tendencies of his own time within the parameters of a well-established iconophile tradition. Indeed, Peter Darby has argued that his commentary on the Temple, written just before 731, was perhaps penned in part in response to Leo III's edict of 730 that resulted in the portrait of Christ being removed from the Chalke Gate of the imperial palace in Constantinople – to which Gregory III responded with a synod in Rome where iconoclasm was formally condemned as heretical and its promoters excommunicated.[50]

Within this tradition Bede considered the function of such visuals as being intended to place "ζώγραφία' [*epigrafia*] a 'living writing' (*viva scriptura*)" before the eyes of the viewer *because* they could produce a feeling of great compunction.[51] In such acts of viewing, a person or event from the past was called to mind in the present, enabling their future significance in the process of salvation to be recalled. Viewing thus enabled imagined movement through time and planes of existence: between past, present and future; between the (tangible, material) human, and the (intangible, uncontainable, immaterial) Divine.

That the carved relief panels of the Anglo-Saxon crosses can be accepted as being understood in this manner is certainly implied by Bede, who refers to the relief carvings of Solomon's Temple as appearing "as if they were coming out of the wall", and to those viewing these reliefs as "no longer learning the words and works of truth extrinsically from others" but having them:

> deeply rooted within themselves, [...] holding them in constant readiness [so that they] can bring forth from their inmost hearts the things that ought to be done and taught.[52]

In other words, the three-dimensional nature of relief carving was understood to enact those necessary processes of viewing imagery: compunction and contemplation.[53] It is, perhaps, no accident that the figure of the Crucified in the cross-head from Rothbury defies the limits of the cross (see Fig. 2). His halo extends over both the outer and inner mouldings that act to outline and emphasise its confines, thus fracturing its shape, and theologically its function as a 'gallows', allowing it to become almost literally the means to life everlasting, crossing boundaries and extending beyond planar surfaces to bring the divine into the realm of the human viewer.

Summary

By exploring the ideas generated by Jennifer O'Reilly all those years ago in relation to the carved images on the high crosses of Anglo-Saxon England, it is possible to see that even if these monuments did not generally function as crucifixes bearing the figure of Christ crucified in the cross-head, they certainly depicted the event – as Christ victorious over death on the cross – in the form of three-dimensional carvings, that were highly painted and multi-media in their presentation. In their placement and the often complex iconographic signifiers employed in their depiction they thus provide clear evidence that the sculptured image of the Crucifixion on the stone cross was understood to be something venerated, liturgically and devotionally. Furthermore, Bede makes it clear that the carvings were understood as painted panels, and so functioned as 'icons'. As relief carvings they thus emerged 'from the wall' to occupy the space inhabited by the viewer – a phenomenon exaggerated by the carvers – bringing the Crucifixion, the means of universal salvation, into the plane of human existence, inspiring compunction and so enabling contemplation of Christ's salvific act on the Cross and its implications: past, present and future.

Abbreviations

ASSAH	Anglo-Saxon Studies in Archaeology and History.
BAA	British Archaeological Association.
CASSS	Corpus of Anglo-Saxon Stone Sculpture.
CCSL	Corpus Christianorum Series Latina.
DLS	*De Locis Sanctis*. Adamnán in Meehan, *Adamnan's De Locis Sanctis*; Bede in Fraipont, *Itineraria et Alia Geographica*, 249–280; trans. Foley, *Biblical Miscellany*, 5–25.
HA	Bede, *Historia Abbatum*, in Grocock and Woods, *Abbots of Wearmouth and Jarrow*, 21–75.
HE	Bede, *Historia Ecclesiastica,* in Colgrave and Mynors, *Bede's Ecclesiastical History*.
JWCI	*Journal of the Warburg and Courtauld Institutes*.
MGH	Monumenta Germaniae Historica.
SLH	Scriptores Latini Hiberniae.
TTH	Translated Texts for Historians.
VC	Adamnán, *Vita Columbae*, in Anderson and Anderson, *Life of Columba*.
VW	*Vita Willibaldi*. in Holder-Egger, *Vitae Willibaldi*, 86–106; trans. Talbot, *Anglo-Saxon Missionaries*, 151–177.

Notes

1. Okasha and O'Reilly, 'An Anglo-Saxon Portable Altar'.
2. Ibid., 37.
3. Bede, *HE* I.26, I.33 (Colgrave and Mynors, *Bede's Ecclesiastical History*, 76–79, 114–117); see discussions in, e.g., Cramp, *Early Northumbrian Sculpture*; Hawkes, 'Iuxta Morem Romanorum'. For an overview, see Mitchell, 'The High Cross', 88–95.
4. Adomnán, *VC* I.45; III.23 (Anderson and Anderson, *Life of Columba*, 306–307; 522–523; Bede, *HE* III.2 (Colgrave and Mynors, *Bede's Ecclesiastial History*, 214–219). Although the battle is recorded in Adomnán's *VC* (I.1), the raising of the cross

is not mentioned; rather the victory is attributed to Columba's intercession (Anderson and Anderson, *Life of Columba*, 198–201). See also Mac Lean, 'King Oswald's Wooden Cross'.

5. Bede, *DLS*, 256; see discussion in Hawkes, 'Anglo-Saxon Legacy'; see also Adomnán, *DLS* 2, 42–47.
6. Holder-Egger, *Vitae Willibaldi*; trans. Talbot, *Anglo-Saxon Missionaries*.
7. See Hawkes, 'Anglo-Saxon Legacy'; Hawkes, 'The Church Triumphant'.
8. Hawkes, 'Anglo-Saxon Legacy'. For further discussion, see Mitchell, 'The High Cross'.
9. Ó Carragáin, 'Christ over the Beasts'; Ó Carragáin, *Ritual and the Rood*, 249, 285.
10. Bailey, *England's Earliest Sculptors*, 23–41.
11. For recent discussion, see Ó Carragáin, 'The Santa Sabina Crucifixion Panel'; see also carnelian intaglio, third to fourth century in the British Museum (1895, 1113.1) which shows only the cross-bar of the cross (Schiller, *Iconography*, fig. 321).
12. For summary, see Bailey, *England's Earliest Sculptors*, 23–41.
13. For a full account, see Rodwell et al., 'The Lichfield Angel', and more recently, Hawkes and Sidebottom, *Derbyshire and Staffordshire*, 302–307, pl. 1, ills. 575–578 (Lichfield 1).
14. Tweddle, *South-East England*, 157, ills. 118 (Reculver 1b); Hawkes, 'Column Fragment'.
15. Hawkes, *The Sandbach Crosses*, 146, 151, figs. 5.7, 6.3; Bailey, *Cheshire and Lancashire*, 100, ills. 250 (Sandbach Market Place 1).
16. Hawkes, 'The Rothbury Cross'; Cramp, *Northumberland and County Durham*, 217–221, pls 211,1206–1207, 212,1210, 213,1213–1216, 213,1218–1219, 214,1220–1221, 214,1223, 215, 1224 (Rothbury 1).
17. Blackwell, 'Bright Eyes'.
18. Hawkes, 'The Rothbury Cross', 77–80; Cramp, *Northumberland and County Durham*, 217–219, 220–221, pl. 211,1206 (Rothbury 1); contra Mitchell, 'The High Cross', 88.
19. Hawkes and Sidebottom, *Derbyshire and Staffordshire*, 105–113, esp. 108–109 (Bakewell 1).
20. Hawkes, *Sandbach Crosses*, 38–46; Bailey, *Cheshire and Lancashire*, 102, 108–109, ills. 251 (Sandbach Market Place 1).

21. For Hexham, see Cramp, *Northumberland and County Durham*, 176–177, pls 173.914 (Hexham 2); for Bradbourne, see Hawkes and Sidebottom, *Derbyshire and Staffordshire*, 147–152, esp. 151 (Bradbourne 1).
22. Wilfrid and Benedict Biscop's first trip to Rome occurred *c.* 653–658.
23. Humiliavit semetipsum factus obediens usque ad mortem, mortem autem crucis. Propter quod et Deus exaltavit illum, et donavit illi nomen, quod est super omne nomen: ut in nomine Jesu omne genu flectatur caelestium, terrestrium et infernorum. I am grateful to Terence O'Reilly for bringing this to my attention.
24. Hurst, *Bede the Venerable*, 8–9; 259.
25. gloriari, nisi in cruce Domini nostri Jesu Christi.
26. Chazelle, *The Crucified God*, 85–95
27. See above, p. 5.
28. Schiller, *Iconography*, 109; Chazelle, *The Crucified God*, 277.
29. Hawkes and Sidebottom, *Derbyshire and Staffordshire*, 74–77.
30. It was included in early Christian art, albeit not in images of the Crucifixions, being preserved in the *c.* 400 apse mosaic of Santa Pudenzia in Rome (Schlatter, 'Interpreting the Mosaic', pl. on 277).
31. Schiller, *Iconography*, 95–97.
32. Et effundam super domum David et super habitatores Hierusalem spiritum gratiae et precum et aspicient ad me quem confixerunt et plangent eum planctu quasi super unigenitum et dolebunt super eum ut doleri solet in morte primogeniti.
33. Et videbit eum omnis oculus, et qui eum pupugerunt.
34. Augustine, *Tractate XXXVI.12 in Iohan. 8.16–18*: sed quoniam bonis et malis in iudicio solus Filius apparebit, in ea forma in qua passus est, et resurrexit, et adscendit in caelum [...] id est, in forma hominis in qua iudicatus est iudicabit, ut etiam illud propheticum impleatur: "Videbunt in quem pupugerunt". (Mayer, *Sancti Aurelii Augustini*, 331; trans. Schaff, *Nicene and Post-Nicene Fathers*, 213). See also Tractate XX1.13 in Mayer, *Sancti Aurelii Augustini*, 219–220.
35. Augustine, *Tractate CXX.2 in Iohann.19.31–35*: "Sed unus militum lancea latus eius aperuit, et continuo exiuit sanguis et aqua". Vigilanti uerbo euangelista usus est, ut non diceret: Latus eius percussit, aut uulnerauit, aut quid aliud; sed: "aperuit";

ut illic quodammodo uitae ostium panderetur, unde sacramenta ecclesiae manauerunt, sine quibus ad uitam quae uera uita est, non intratur. (Mayer, *Sancti Aurelii Augustini*, 661; trans. Schaff, *Nicene and Post-Nicene Fathers*, 434).

36. Chazelle, *The Crucified God*, 85–95.
37. Ó Carragáin, *Ritual and the Rood*, 95–106; Webster and Backhouse, *The Making of England*, 180–183, cat.141.
38. Lang, *York and Eastern Yorkshire*, 146–148; Hawkes, 'Mary and the Cycle of Resurrection', 254–256, 259.
39. E.g., San Vincenzo al Volturno, Italy, 826–843; Prayerbook of Charles the Bald 846–869, Munich, Residenz, Schatzkammer, fols 38v–39r (Schiller, *Iconography*, figs. 346, 354); see also Mitchell, 'The High Cross', fig. 7:15; Chazelle, *The Crucified Christ*, 155–158.
40. E.g., Stuttgart Psalter, 820–839, Württemburgische Landesbibliothek, Stuttgart, Bibl. Fol. 23; engraved crystal, mid-ninth century; Otto von Weissenburg Gospel Harmony, *c*. 868, Vienna, Österreichische Nationalbibliothek (Schiller, *Iconography*, figs. 355, 361, 363).
41. Chazelle, *The Crucified Christ*, 124.
42. Ibid., 118–131.
43. Mitchell, The High Cross', 95.
44. Hawkes, 'Stones of the North', 45–50.
45. Bede, *HE* I.25 (Colgrave and Mynors, *Ecclesiastical History*, 75–77); Bede, *HA* 7 (Grocock and Wood, *History of the Abbots*, 36–39).
46. Meyvaert, 'Bede and the Church Paintings'.
47. Bede, *De Templo* 2.824–843: Si eidem legi contrarium non fuit in eodem mari scalpturas histriatas […] quomodo legi contrarium putabatur si historias sanctorum ac martyrum Christi sculpamus siue pingamus in tabulis qui per custodiam diuinae legis ad gloriam meruerunt aeternae retributionis attingere (Hurst, *Bedae Venerabilis*, 212–213; trans. Connolly, *Bede*, 91–92.
48. Bede, *De Templo* 2.832–833: Si enim licebat serpentem exaltari aeneum in ligno quem aspicientes filii Israhel uiuerent, cur non licet exaltationem domini saluatoris in cruce qua mortem uicit ad memoriam fidelibus depingendo reduci uel etiam alia eius miracula et sanationes quibus de eodem mortis auctore mirabiliter triumphauit cum horum aspectus multum saepe compunctionis

soleat praestare contuentibus (Hurst, *Bedae Venerabilis Opera*, 212; trans. Connolly, *Bede*, 91).

49. Gregory I, *Sereno episcopi Massiliensi*: Et si quis imagines facere voluerit, minime prohibe, adorare vero imagines omnimodis devita. Sed hoc sollicite fraternitas tuo ammoneat, ut ex visione rei gestae ardorem compunctionis percipant et in adoratione solius omnipotentis sanctae trinitatis humiliter prosternantur. (Ewald and Hartman, *Gregorii I papae*, 271; trans. Martyn, *Letters of Gregory* 3, 746).
50. Darby, 'Bede'.
51. Bede, *De Templo* II.832–33: "Nam et pictura Graece ζωγραφία, id est uiua scriptura, uocatur", in Hurst, *Bedae Venerabilis Opera*, 213; trans. Connolly, *Bede* 2.19:10, 91.
52. Bede, *De Templo* I.1509–1515: Quae uidelicet uirtutes cum in tantam electis consuetudinem uenerint ut uelut naturaliter eis esse uideantur insitae quid aliud quam picturae domus domini prominentes quasi de pariete exeunt quia uerba et opera ueritatis non adhuc ab aliis extrinsecus discunt sed ut sibimet infixa radicitus parata semper ab intimis cordis quae sunt agenda siue docenda proferunt (Hurst, *Bedae Venerabilis Opera*, 184–185; trans. Connolly, *Bede* 1.14:2, 54, following Darby, 'Bede', 419).
53. For overview see, e.g., Baker, *The Evangelists in Insular Culture*.

Bibliography

Anderson, Alan O. and Marjorie O. Anderson. (eds./trans.), *Adamnan's Life of Columba* (London: Nelson, 1961).

Baker, N. *The Evangelists in Insular Culture, c.600–c.800 AD*, 2 vols (Unpublished PhD Thesis, University of York, 2012).

Bailey, Richard. *England's Earliest Sculptors* (Toronto: Pontifical Institute of Medieval Studies, 1996).

——. *Cheshire and Lancashire*, CASSS 9 (Oxford: OUP, 2010).

Blackwell, Alice. 'Bright Eyes: Recreating Medieval Sculpture', https://blog.nms.ac.uk/2012/06/05/bright-eyes-recreating-medieval-sculpture/ (Accessed 8 April 2018).

Chazelle, Celia. *The Crucified God in the Carolingian Era: Theology and Art of Christ's Passion* (Cambridge: CUP, 2001).

Colgrave, Bertram and R.A.B. Mynors. (eds.), *Bede's Ecclesiastical History of the English People* (Oxford: Clarendon Press, 1969).

Connolly, Sean. (trans.) *Bede: On the Temple*, with an introduction by Jennifer O'Reilly, TTH 21 (Liverpool: Liverpool University Press, 1995).

Cramp, Rosemary. *Early Northumbrian Sculpture*. Jarrow Lecture (Jarrow: Friends of Jarrow Church, 1965). 23

——. *Northumberland and County Durham*, CASSS 1 (Oxford: OUP, 1984).

Darby, Peter. 'Bede, Iconoclasm and the Temple of Solomon', *Early Medieval Europe* 21.4 (2013), 390–421.

Ewald, Paul and Hartman, Ludwig M. (eds.), *Gregorii I papae registrum epistolarum*, MGH: Epistolae 2 (Berlin: Weidmann, 1899).

Foley, W. Trent. (ed./trans.), *Bede, A Biblical Miscellany*. TTH 28 (Liverpool: Liverpool University Press, 1999).

Fraipont, J. (ed.), *Itineraria et Alia Geographica*, CCSL 175 (Turnhout: Brepols, 1965).

Christopher Grocock and Ian N. Wood. (eds./trans.), *Abbots of Wearmouth and Jarrow* (Oxford: OUP, 2013).

Hawkes, Jane. 'The Rothbury Cross: An Iconographic Bricolage', *Gesta* 35.1 (1996), 73–90.

——. 'Mary and the Cycle of Resurrection: The Iconography of the Hovingham Panel', in Michael Spearman and John Higgitt (eds.), *The Age of Migrating Ideas*. Second International Conference on Insular Art: Edinburgh 1991 (Edinburgh: National Museum of Scotland), 1993), 254–260.

——. *The Sandbach Crosses: Sign and Significance in Anglo-Saxon Sculpture* (Dublin: Four Courts Press, 2002).

——. '*Iuxta Morem Romanorum*: Stone and Sculpture in Anglo-Saxon England', in Catherine Karkov and George Hardin Brown (eds.), *Anglo-Saxon Styles* (Albany: SUNY, 2003), 69–100.

——. 'The Anglo-Saxon Legacy', in Elizabeth Hartley, Jane Hawkes and Martin Henig (eds.), *Constantine the Great: York's Roman Emperor* (London: Lund Humphries, 2006), 104–114.

——. 'The Church Triumphant: The Figural Columns of Early Ninth-Century Anglo-Saxon England', in Sally Crawford and Helena Hamerow (eds.), *Form and Order in the Anglo-Saxon World, AD 600–1100*. ASSAH 16 (Oxford: Oxford University School of Archaeology, 2009), 29–42.

——. 'Stones of the North: Sculpture in Northumbria in the "Age of Bede"', in Jeremy Ashbee and Julian Luxford (eds.), *Newcastle and Northumberland: Roman and Medieval Architecture and Art*, BAA Conference Transactions 36 (Leeds: Maney Publishing, 2013), 34–53.

——. and Philip Sidebottom. *Derbyshire and Staffordshire*, CASSS 13 (Oxford: OUP: 2018).

Holder-Egger, Oswald. (ed.), *Vitae Willibaldi Episcopi Eichstentensis*, in Societas Aperiendis Fontibus (ed.), *Inde ab Anno Christi Quingentesimo usque ad Annum Millesimum et Quingentesimum*, MGH: Scriptorum 15.1 (Stuttgart: Anton Hiersemann, repr. 1992), 86–106.

Hurst, David. (ed.), *Bedae Venerabilis Opera*, CCSL 119A (Turnhout: Brepols, 1969).

——. (trans.), *Bede the Venerable. Excerpts from the Works of Saint Augustine on the Letters of the Blessed Apostle Paul* (Kalamazoo, MI: Cistercian Publications, 1999).

Lang, James. *York and Eastern Yorkshire*, CASSS 3 (Oxford: OUP, 1991).

Little, Charles T. and Timothy B. Husband. *Europe in the Middle Ages: The Metropolitan Museum of Art* (New York: Metropolitan Museum of Art, 1987). 24

Mac Lean, Douglas. 'King Oswald's Wooden Cross at Heavenfield in Context', in Catherine Karkov, Michael Ryan and Robert Farrell (eds.), *The Insular Tradition* (Albany, NY: SUNY, 1997), 79–98.

Martyn, John R. C. (trans.), *The Letters of Gregory the Great*, 3 vols (Toronto, 2004).

Mayer, A. (ed.), *Sancti Avrelii Avgvstini in Iohannis Evangelivm tractatvs CXXIV*, CCSL 36 (Turnhout: Brepols, 1954).

Meehan, Denis. (ed./trans.), *Adamnan's De Locis Sanctis*. SLH 3 (Dublin: Dublin Institute for Advanced Studies, 1958).

Meyvaert, Paul. 'Bede and the Church Paintings at Wearmouth-Jarrow', *Anglo-Saxon England* 8 (1979), 63–77.

Mitchell, John. 'The High Cross and Monastic Strategies in Eighth-century Northumbria', in Paul Binski and William Noel (eds.), *New Offerings, Ancient Treasures: Studies in Medieval Art for George Henderson* (Cambridge: CUP, 2001), 88–114.

Ó Carragáin, Éammon. 'Christ over the Beasts and the Agnus Dei: Two Multivalent Panels on the Ruthwell and Bewcastle Crosses', in Paul E. Szarmach with Virginia. D. Oggins (eds.), *Sources of Anglo-Saxon Culture* (Kalamazoo, WM: Medieval Institute Publications, 1986), 377–403.

——. *Ritual and the Rood: Liturgical Images and the Old English Poems of the Dream of the Rood Tradition* (London: The British Library and Toronto University Press, 2005).

——. 'The Santa Sabina Crucifixion Panel: "Between two living creatures you will be known" on Good Friday, at "Hierusalem" in fifth-century Rome', in Eric Cambridge and Jane Hawkes (eds.), *Crossing Boundaries: Interdisciplinary Approaches to the Art, Material Culture, Language and Literature of the Early Medieval World* (Oxford: Oxbow Books, 2017), 69–77.

Okasha, Elizabeth and Jennifer O'Reilly. 'An Anglo-Saxon Portable Altar: Inscription and Iconography', *JWCI* 47 (1984), 32–51.

Plummer, John., J. Russell and C. Pierce, Jr. (eds.), *In August Company: The Collections of the Pierpont Morgan Library* (New York: Pierpont Morgan Library, 1993).

Rodwell, Warwick, Jane Hawkes, Rosemary Cramp and Emily Howe. 'The Lichfield Angel: A Spectacular Anglo-Saxon Painted Sculpture', *The Antiquaries Journal* 88 (2008), 1–60.

Schaff, Philip. (trans.), *Nicene and Post-Nicene Fathers of the Christian Church*, vol. 7 (repr. Grand Rapids, MI, 1978).

Schiller, Gertrud. *Christian Iconography, 2: The Passion of Jesus Christ*, trans. Janet Seligman (London: Lund Humphries, 1972).

Schlatter, Fredric W. 'Interpreting the Mosaic of Santa Pudenziana', *Vigiliae Christianae* 46.3 (1992), 276–295.

Talbot, Charles H. *The Anglo-Saxon Missionaries in Germany* (New York: Sheed and Ward, 1954).

Tweddle, Dominic. *South-East England*, CASSS 4 (Oxford: OUP, 1995).

Webster, Leslie and Janet Backhouse. (eds.), *The Making of England: Anglo-Saxon Art and Culture, AD 600–900* (London: British Museum, 1991).

Williamson, Paul. *Medieval Ivory Carvings: Early Christian to Romanesque* (London: V&A Publishing, 2010).

List of illustrations

Figure 1. The Cluny Altar. Anglo-Saxon portable altar, late tenth century. Musée de Cluny, Paris (Photo: Musée de Cluny, Musée national du Moyen Âge, Paris.).

Figure 2. The Crucifixion. Rothbury cross-head (Northumberland), late eighth century. The Great North Museum, Newcastle upon Tyne (Photo: Jane Hawkes).

Figure 3. The Ruthwell Cross viewed from below (Dumfriess and Galloway), mid-eighth century. St Cuthbert's Church, Ruthwell (Photo: Jane Hawkes).

Figure 4. Obelisk now standing before St Peter's, Rome (Photo: Jane Hawkes).

Figure 5. Rupertus Cross. Anglo-Saxon, later eighth century. Bischofshofen, Pongau (Salzburger Raum), Austria (Replica, Jarrow Museum, Tyne and Wear; Photo: Jane Hawkes).

Figure 6. Crucifixion. Wooden Panel, Doors of Santa Sabina, Rome, *c*. 430–432 (Photo: Jane Hawkes).

Figure 7. The Lichfield Angel. Part of the shrine of St Chad, early ninth century. Lichfield Cathedral (Photo: Courtesy of Dean and Chapter of Lichfield Cathedral).

Figure 8. Ascension of Christ. Fragment of Reculver Column, early ninth century. Canterbury Cathedral (Photo: Jane Hawkes).

Figure 9. Crucifixion. Bakewell cross-head (Derbyshire), early ninth century. All Saints' Church (Photo: Jane Hawkes).

Figure 10. Crucifixion. Hexham (Northumberland), mid-eighth century. Abbey Church of St Andrew (Photo: copyright Corpus of Anglo-Saxon Stone Sculpture, photographer T. Middlemass).

Figure 11. Majestas over crux gemmata with Manus Dei above. San Stefano Rotondo, Rome, *c*. 643–649 (Photo: Jane Hawkes).

Figure 12. Crucifixion. Bradbourne (Derbyshire), early ninth century. All Saints' Church (Photo: Jane Hawkes).

Figure 13a. The Bakewell Cross. Early ninth century. All Saints' Church: The West Face. (Photos: copyright Corpus of Anglo-Saxon Stone Sculpture, photographers K. Jukes and D. Craig).

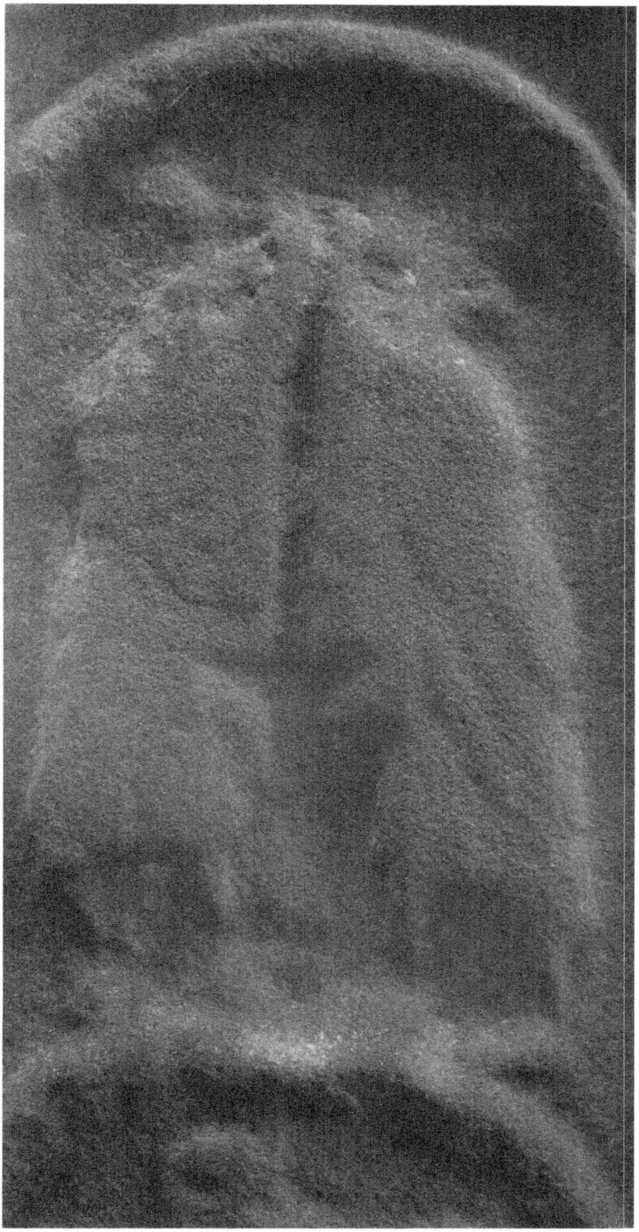

Figure 13b. The Bakewell Cross. Early ninth century. All Saints' Church: Pair of Adoring Figures. (Photos: copyright Corpus of Anglo-Saxon Stone Sculpture, photographers K. Jukes and D. Craig).

Figure 14a. The Visitation. Ruthwell, Dumfriess, mid-eighth century. St Cuthbert's Church (Photo: Jane Hawkes).

Figure 14b. The Visitation. Hovingham, North Yorkshire, early ninth century. All Saints' Church (Photo: Jane Hawkes).

Figure 15. The Bradbourne Cross. Early ninth century. All Saints' Church (Photo: Jane Hawkes).

Figure 16. The Damned in Hell. Rothbury cross, late eighth century. All Saints' Church (Photo: Jane Hawkes).

Printed in Great Britain
by Amazon

34066962R00030